NORTHAMPTONSHIRE
A century in photographs

Published jointly by
Northamptonshire Federation
of Women's Institutes and

Countryside Books

COUNTRYSIDE BOOKS
3 Catherine Road
Newbury, Berkshire

ISBN 1 85306 575 7

Designed by Graham Whiteman

Produced through MRM Associates Ltd., Reading
Printed by J. W. Arrowsmith Ltd., Bristol

FOREWORD

⚬⚬

Northamptonshire is a long thin county, criss-crossed by motorways and major roads, but turn off these roads and venture into the countryside, to where lovely villages with warm sandstone cottages nestle, like little pockets of England that don't seem to have ever changed.

Yet this has been a century of change. Towns have spread out into the countryside, our houses have comforts never dreamed of by our great grandparents, villages have become the homes for commuters rather than local labourers, and the motor car has spread its influence into every corner of the land.

It all seems so distant from us today – the clip-clopping of horses along the village street, the workers in the fields, the humming of bees on unpolluted air, children laughing and playing as they help bring in the hay – like something from a Thomas Hardy novel or a Constable painting. Now, at the turn of the Millennium, man and woman, can travel the world and even venture into space.

These photographs provide an insight into old and new, with each photograph from the early years of the 20th century matched by another from its end. You will perhaps be surprised at how often continuity has been more important than change, as villages have absorbed the new but retained their sense of identity.

Thanks must go to the members of the Women's Institutes throughout the county who have worked so hard to produce a 'matching pair' of photographs of historic interest.

One wonders what life in our Northamptonshire villages will be like in 100 years time, but for today you are invited to enjoy the memories that this book will bring.

Christine Farmer
Federation Chairman

Ashley is a small village on a quiet country road and when this photograph was taken in about 1900 it was self sufficient with a school, shop, post office and rectory. Village people had come out of their houses in Main Street, and the carrier's cart was standing ready to carry goods and messages to town. The old butcher's shop is in the right foreground and the cottages are thatched.

4 *(Ann Dancer, Gwen Maguire – Ashley with Weston by Welland WI. Photo courtesy of Dr Aubrey Stewart.)*

Today the road and pavements are much better maintained, and cars proliferate. On the right the village hall and council houses have replaced the shop and thatched cottages. The tumbledown mass at the left centre has been removed to create a green approach to the old people's bungalows. The village has a decidedly more prosperous appearance!
(Ann Dancer, Gwen Maguire – Ashley with Weston by Welland WI)

Barby has remained a rural community, much as it was in 1907 when the Pytchley Hunt met on the Rugby to Daventry road at the junction of Rectory Lane. In the 1980s the Hunt was banned from meeting here by the parish council. The properties in the background all survive today (*inset*) and the hedge on the left surrounds allotments, still popular with villagers. The now metalled road has wide grass verges, and the poles bear electricity cables, installed after 1945.
(*Eileen Dawson – Barby WI*)

Barton Seagrave has been transformed since the 1920s, when the building with its gable end facing us was the village smithy. Today *(inset)* it is a garage, while the post box on the right stands before a new purpose-built post office. The road then was just a rough track turning to the right past the church, but now cuts straight through where the row of old cottages stood. *(Sheilagh Brooks – Barton Seagrave WI)*

In about 1920, the carrier's cart stands outside Boughton's oldest thatched estate workers' cottages, which include the then inn (there were three at that time), the Griffin. The cart was the lifeline for villagers each Wednesday and Saturday to Northampton's market. The stone archway was part of Boughton's 18th century Follies, and the entrance to the Hall. In the foreground is the village green elm, known as the Cross Tree.
(Sylvia Lovell, Norma Pearson – Boughton WI)

The arch was removed in the 1960s and now the piers bear statues of a lion and griffin, the heraldic supporters of the coat of arms of the Earl of Strafford. Four of the old cottages are garages and flats, and the whole block has been bulwarked. The old elms in the park and on the green have gone, and a chestnut now graces the green.

(Sylvia Lovell, Norma Pearson – Boughton WI)

Braunston, due to its location on the crossroads of the Grand Union and Oxford Canals, was a mixture of working narrow boats and agriculture when this picture was taken in the 1920s. There were many shops and at least eight pubs – from the left we can see here a shoemaker's, a barber's, a draper's, a butcher's, a newsagent and tobacconist's, and behind the railings was a cottage home for poor people, with an isolation hospital.
(Jackie Green, Gillian Powell – Braunston WI)

Today the canals bring tourists and the village is popular with walkers, while there is still some agriculture. The 'home' is now the post office, and the trees that could be seen in the background, part of a large wood, have gone to make way for council housing.
(Gillian Powell – Braunston WI)

Braybrooke is a small village three miles south east of Market Harborough, in a valley bisected by the River Jordan. Even today the population is only about 380. This view along the Arthingworth Road looks north towards the Swan Inn in the early 1920s, when a horse and trap was a common means of transport along the rough roads.

12 *(Freda Goodman – Braybrooke WI)*

Much has changed since then. Houses have been demolished to provide sites for new buildings, or combined to provide more spacious accommodation. The cottages below the Swan Inn were demolished to provide car parking. Even the road has been renamed, to become Griffin Road!

(Freda Goodman – Braybrooke WI)

Bugbrooke looked very different in 1900, as this photograph shows. On the left was the village bakery, where on a Sunday people would take their Yorkshire puddings to be baked. The inn, the Waggon and Horses, faced a row of thatched cottages across the street – quiet enough for children to pose for the photographer without risk!

14   *(Eileen Sargent – Bugbrooke WI)*

Today only four buildings remain from that earlier scene, giving the impression that the population of Bugbrooke may have diminished, but the opposite is the case as the village is still growing with over 2,500 inhabitants. The thatched cottages have gone, and so has the public house – and horses and carts have been replaced by horse power of a very different kind.
(Eileen Sargent – Bugbrooke WI)

This old photograph was labelled 'The Group – 1925', and shows the May Queen and her attendants in white, some with crowns of flowers or carrying posies for the May Day celebrations. Miss Miriam Groome, their teacher from 1913 to 1938, is with them, and the shadow of the maypole can be seen in the foreground. There were then about 80 houses in the village.

(Christine Foulger – Chelveston-cum-Caldecott WI)

THE GROUP, CALDECOTT

Only the tree and the grass bank remain the same for this 'group' of villagers and the Mother and Toddlers Club. The old almshouses and Pastures Farm Cottages fell into disrepair and were replaced in about 1985, while the population has grown to about 380. We have lost the shop and post office, but still have a popular pub!

(Christine Foulger – Chelveston-cum-Caldecott WI)

In 1901 the Chacombe Whitsun Club lined up outside the 17th century village pub, the George and Dragon, prior to parading round the village. To the right of the pub the lane leads to the church. The Whitsun Club has long since disbanded, but Chacombe is still a very public spirited village.

18 *(Betty Cameron, Philippa Foord-Kelcey – Chacombe WI)*

THE GEORGE AND DRAGON, CHACOMBE

The George and Dragon has changed very little, though the thatched roof is now tiled. Chacombe is still a pretty village with many houses and cottages as old as the pub, some still thatched, and in-filling has been discreet in the centre of the village. Two small new estates have added to the size of the village, which supports a post office, school and village hall.
(Jill Deacon, Philippa Foord-Kelcey – Chacombe WI)

GOLD STREET, CLIPSTON

Up until 1903, there was a working windmill in Clipston and a range of trades and crafts such as bakers, tailors, brickmakers, butchers, a blacksmith, shoemakers, a wheelwright, a saddler – even a milliner and a music seller! In the 1920s when this picture was taken, it was still a self-sufficient village with most of the inhabitants working locally and agriculture the main source of employment.

(Doreen Tebbutt, Rose Anderson – Clipston WI)

Today most people travel outside the village to work, but Clipston still has a thriving village school, two pubs, a few local businesses and farms. The cottages on the left, where the Co-op shop was built in 1937, are no longer thatched, and sadly the green is no longer there, but there is a feeling of continuity with the past and those who walked the same streets we walk today. *(Rose Anderson – Clipston WI)*

IVY COTTAGE, COLD ASHBY

In 1900, the solid figures of Mr and Mrs Watts posed outside Ivy Cottage. Mr Watts was a builder and he is seated in his working cart. At that time the village had its own school, post office and shop, all now gone, as have the right-hand cottage and thatched extension which once buttressed Ivy Cottage.

(Jane Simon – Cold Ashby WI)

Ivy Cottage, Cold Ashby

Ivy Cottage today is being renovated, and kept to its original features. Naturally many things have changed around it over the years but the community spirit of the village is still strong. The introduction of the A14, with access less than a mile away, has increased the volume of traffic but also made local towns easier to reach than in the days of mule and cart.
(Jane Simon – Cold Ashby WI)

This view down Main Street in the early part of the century shows the Plough Inn on the right, and, top right, the bakery. Across the road was the old workhouse yard, a reminder of harder days when unemployment or illness could bring the shame of the workhouse to a family. The Grand Union Canal divides Cosgrove in two and in those days it was a working canal.

24 *(Sue Richards – Cosgrove WI)*

Today the canal brings tourists. The handrail beside the steps to the towpath can be seen here, though the cars obscure the view of the horse tunnel, a quick cut through to the Barley Mow, Cosgrove's only remaining public house. The Plough is now a private house, and the bakery a small hotel. To the left, the road leads to Cosgrove Park, a leisure park built on the site of old gravel pits, which has brought the greatest change to Cosgrove village.
(Sue Richards – Cosgrove WI)

25

STATION HOUSE, CRANFORD

Cranford's railway station was opened for goods traffic on 21st February 1866 and later that same year, for passengers. For the first half of the 20th century it was an important part of village life, in the days when private motor cars were relatively scarce. (*Sandra Naylor – Cranford WI*)

STATION HOUSE, CRANFORD

Beeching's axe fell on many rural stations in the 1960s, and Cranford was closed in November 1961. It was then sold and the station, built of local stone, has today become a beautiful private house, still retaining many of the original features including the platform.
(Sandra Naylor – Cranford WI)

The garage opened in 1918 and stood on this site until 1938, and Mr John Marson had the first village taxi. Before the 1940s Crick's only employment was agriculture and villagers did not travel far. After the garage closed the site became a lay-by, and in the 1980s an estate of 'executive-type' houses was built *(inset)*, totally altering the appearance of the village.

28 *(Jean Garner – Crick WI)*

These cottages may have been some of the first built by forest workers in Deanshanger, using material from the nearby brick kiln and stone quarry. It was 'Little London', with a sweet shop and a thatched public house, the Rose and Crown. Today *(inset)* gone are the cottages selling home cured bacon, black puddings and pillow lace, replaced by supermarkets, and cars galore!
(Evelyn Heppinstall – Deanshanger WI)

A view down Broad Street, Earls Barton in about 1910. Just visible on the left in this peaceful scene are two shoeworkers in their long aprons. The white building near them is the Battle of Inkerman beerhouse, and on the skyline can be seen All Saints parish church and the Baptist chapel.

(Joyce Palmer, Maurice Palmer – Earls Barton WI)

Broad Street, Earls Barton

Earls Barton is still a shoemaking village, with three factories. The level of Broad Street has been raised, and the library now fronts a pleasant green area. Churchill Road to the right leads to extensive modern developments – the population now exceeds 5,500 and shopping and public amenities are therefore good.
(Joyce Palmer, Maurice Palmer – Earls Barton WI)

The main road through Great Doddington in 1910 was a quiet thoroughfare – was the man with the pails carrying milk, or water home from the well? On the left, people sit on the steps of a shop, and the buildings on the right include the post office, with a barn nearest the photographer.

32 *(Audrey Whinnett – Gt Doddington WI)*

For safety's sake, today's photograph had to be taken from a slightly different position! The scene on the left is largely unchanged, but new houses have replaced most of the old buildings on the right. However, the wall of the barn, which is still in use, remains.

(Audrey Whinnett – Gt Doddington WI)

Many Great Houghton characters gathered in front of Ye Olde Cherry Tree Inn for this photo just before the First World War. They include the then proprietor, Sam Garratt. A few years later, Mr Seaton took over and became the village carrier, keeping his horse behind the pub.

34 *(Margaret Irons – Gt Houghton WI)*

Ye Olde Cherry Tree, Great Houghton

The inn has been at the heart of village life throughout the century, including during the Second World War when the Home Guard met there in the skittle room. Today the exterior has changed very little though much has altered inside – no longer do they go down to the cellar to fetch the beer from the barrels and the skittle room is now a cosy restaurant.
(Eileen Ashdown – Gt Houghton WI)

St Peter's church at Greatworth is situated in what was called Church Row. Descendants of those who lived in these little cottages still live in the village and recall that with no back gardens, washing had to be hung on lines on the bank across the lane. The cottages were demolished before the Second World War.

36   *(Walter Stageman via Greatworth WI)*

After the war, the land was made over to the church and the churchyard extended – unfortunately the cellars were not filled in, as a gravedigger discovered in the 1950s. The cottages to the right survived as part of the Manor Estate, and were given to their tenants in the 1960s after Mrs Dora Hannary's death, a link with the past along Church Row.
(Walter Stageman via Greatworth WI)

In the 1920s Greens Norton, near Towcester, was a sleepy little village. The only vehicle to be seen is believed to be the First World War ambulance purchased by a local man and converted to serve as the local 'bus' – affectionately known as 'the hen house'! Most villagers found employment in and around the village.

38 *(Margaret Shelley – Greens Norton WI)*

Many of today's villagers commute to Northampton or Milton Keynes or even further afield and thatched roofs have given way to tiles – though recently two cottages have had their thatch replaced. The building with bay windows is still a shop – now minus its iron railings and picket fence.

(Margaret Shelley – Greens Norton WI)

At the beginning of the 20th century most of the old stone, thatched roof cottages in Grendon were 'two up and two down' with no mod cons and only a patch of garden. Many of the men worked their own allotments, to the right on this photograph, to grow food for the family.

40 *(Isabel Gillett – Grendon WI)*

MAIN ROAD, GRENDON

The cottages on the left were replaced by a bungalow some years ago – though continuity was ensured as the owner had been born in one of the cottages. The land on the right is now a close of five houses, built in 1973, and the village playing field, which replaced the allotments. Village homes have been modernised and are far more comfortable for their inhabitants than a century ago.
(Isabel Gillett – Grendon WI)

This picture of Gretton was taken in about 1921. To the right is the White Hart, one of the oldest public houses in the village and where skittles were played. The little wooden building was a general stores, and behind was a bakehouse. Next to it was another pub, the Fox.

(Elizabeth Jordan, Sheila Macadam – Gretton WI)

Still recognisable, much has changed by the green. The old bakehouse and the Fox became private houses, while the White Hart closed in 1931, becoming a general stores and newsagent's. The war memorial was erected in 1925, originally with a seat around it. Schoolchildren have, over the years, planted the green with daffodils and Gretton has stayed a friendly village with a good sense of community.

(Elizabeth Jordan, Sheila Macadam – Gretton WI)

Hargrave Village Shop

In 1920, when the village was mainly agricultural, the shop, one of three in Hargrave, sold groceries, confectionery and hardware. Now the shop is a house, there is one pub, a farm shop and a post office for three hours weekly, and Hargrave has become a commuter village. Eva Hills *(left)* lived her whole life here – Yasmin and her generation are likely to go far afield.

44   *(Hilary How, Hilda Rawlings – Hargrave WI)*

The Old House on the A428 Northampton to Rugby road has changed little since 1918 with the sundial still in evidence today (*inset*). Other things have changed though. There were nine tenant farmers, now there are three and few villagers find their employment locally. Many farm buildings are now barn conversions, and estate cottages have been sold. The volume of traffic has increased somewhat!
(*Liz Smith – Harlestone WI*)

In the 1920s there were few cars to disturb the peace of the main street through Harpole – this one appears to have been abandoned in the middle of the road! For many years the main employment for village men was outwork shoemaking and farming, and few travelled far from home, with perhaps an occasional visit to Northampton four miles away.

46 *(Olive Minney – Harpole Evening WI)*

Like many other villages in the vicinity of Northampton, today Harpole is under threat from the county town's expansion and from infill modern development. It is fortunate that parts of the village retain a rural atmosphere centering on the parish church and with several active farms surviving within the locality.
(Avril Judge – Harpole Evening WI)

Main Street in Holcot at the turn of the 20th century boasted a church, a school and a pub, as well as the Town Well from which many local people drew their water. On the left in this view are the Church Institute, the adjoining cottage and school. The three boys are standing outside what was the bakehouse.

48 *(P. Wilson, J. Mould – Holcot WI)*

MAIN STREET, HOLCOT

During the 1960s Main Street was widened and raised to accommodate modern day traffic. The school closed in 1964 and it and the Institute were pulled down in 1970. Successful fundraising by the villagers meant that the site was purchased for use as a village green. Also gone are cottages on the right of the road, though the bakehouse has survived as a private house.
(P. Wilson, J. Mould – Holcot WI)

IRCHESTER HIGH STREET

On the left in this view of Irchester earlier in the century is the library then newly built by the Carnegie Trust. Houses and the Co-op shop lead to the Manor House (behind the wall) and to St Katherine's church. On the right is a draper's shop, the sign of which can just be seen. The farm cart is probably on its way from Lower Farm.

(Geraldine Hunt – Irchester WI)

The modern day removal of buildings means that the church and the entrance to School Hill can be more clearly seen, while alterations have been made to the library entrance to facilitate wheelchair use. There has also been some loss of buildings on the right, though some look much the same, including the old draper's shop, now owned by the St John Ambulance.
(Geraldine Hunt – Irchester WI)

Such a quiet country scene for these children of the 1920s, in a village in which agriculture still predominated and the horse and cart was the normal form of travel. You can just see a cart on the green, to the left of the standing girl.
(Barbara Marlow – Kilsby WI)

That country road is now the A361 leading to the M1 and M6, the A14 and DIRFT (the Daventry International Rail Freight Terminal nearby). White lines have replaced horse manure and the proliferation of road signs and housing now obscure the view of the church. The only enduring features are the green, a little narrower, and the old farmhouse, now a modernised residence. *(Gillian Mason – Kilsby WI)*

 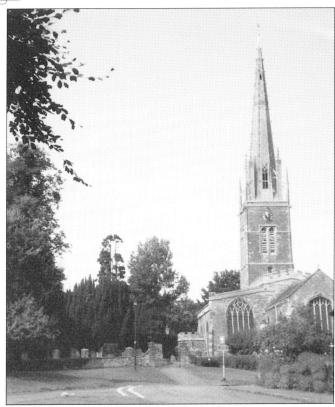

Early in the 20th century the view of the church of St Peter and St Paul was partly obscured by large trees, though the full beauty of the spire could be seen. Today *(right)* the view is much clearer and the church is the focal point of the village green. Though still agricultural, King's Sutton is one of the few villages with a station and many local people commute to work by train or by the M40 nearby.

(Valerie Allen, Pauline Barber – King's Sutton WI)

54

Traffic statistics reveal the greatest measure of the century's changes, for instead of a mere 20 carts, Kislingbury High Street is now *(inset)* assailed by some 4,000 motorised vehicles daily. Gone since 1905 are the thatch and the corn ricks, the farmer on horseback and the village carrier. He never had need of painted white lines to keep his van in lane.
(Ruth Ward – Kislingbury WI)

55

MAIN STREET, LITTLE HARROWDEN

In 1917 Little Harrowden was a largely self-sufficient community of mainly farmworkers – today only one villager makes his living in this way. Others worked in the village iron foundry. The Main Street contained a shop selling village-made bicycles, a thriving chapel, a bakehouse and other shops.

(Mr R. Coles, Joyce Tucker – The Harrowdens WI)

The old iron foundry has gone now, and the chapel is derelict. The shops and bakehouse became a Co-op, then our village hall. The Ten O'Clock has swallowed up a butcher's shop and several old cottages had to make way for a bungalow and the post office – now our only shop. But in its own way the village continues to thrive and still supports a happy and successful school.
(Joyce Tucker – The Harrowdens WI)

LOIS WEEDON

Yes, we still think of the village as Lois Weedon, though over the years its name has been gradually officially accepted as Weedon Lois. That is perhaps one of the major bureaucratic changes of the century, though new housing has expanded the village considerably. Even just looking down the hill towards the church today *(inset)* several new houses occupy the old farmyard and the barn has been converted for accommodation.
(Sheila French, Jennifer Liversidge – Lois Weedon & Weston WI)

Long Buckby's population has doubled since 1900, to 4,000 today after rapid expansion in the 1970s. There were village based farming, wool and shoe industries, but now most people commute to work. Robinson's handcart, delivering greengrocery to the door, is just one of the local services long gone from those days when all carts were hand or horse drawn, and when everyone except the wealthy shopped, probably daily, in the village.
(Joyce Sharp – Long Buckby WI)

59

CROSS STREET, MOULTON

Moulton, situated just five miles from the centre of Northampton, has always had a strong village identity. It is an ancient village, traditionally relying on agriculture but embracing the availability of out-work in the lacemaking and shoemaking industries. This view along Cross Street in the early part of the 20th century gives a glimpse of bustling life, with shops, pub and tradesmen.

(Mary Sheldon – Moulton WI)

CROSS STREET, MOULTON

Despite modern housing estates and considerable industrial development, Moulton has kept its community spirit alive, with a carefully preserved conservation area at its heart. The left hand side of Cross Street has retained nearly all its original cottages. The other side of the road has seen much demolition, but building has been in accordance with conservation requirements, blending the charm of earlier centuries with the demands of modern life.
(Mary Sheldon – Moulton WI)

Captured on camera in a corner of Heyford Green were the village's first motor bus and, still a rarity in the 1920s, a private motor car. These were so few and far between that people used to go up to the A5 to watch for them going by and wave to the drivers! In the 1950s the bus fare return to Northampton was one shilling and threepence (about 7p in decimal currency).

(Judy Armitage, Sheila Masters – Nether Heyford WI)

There is now a Stagecoach double-decker to Northampton almost hourly, as well as a single-decker A1 bus through from Daventry. The fare is nearly £2 return. Cars and vans now abound and the photographer would have difficulty finding such a quiet scene. New housing has doubled the population of the village. But the Green, five acres of it, is still there.
(Maureen Wright, Sheila Masters – Nether Heyford WI)

These two little boys seem to have been sent to collect a small can of milk from one of the nearby farms or smallholdings, which then employed most of the men in Paulerspury. Others would cycle daily to the foundry in Towcester or to Wolverton carriage works. Just down the street behind the boys stands the village school, with the headmaster's house attached.

(Mollie Dunkley – Paulerspury WI)

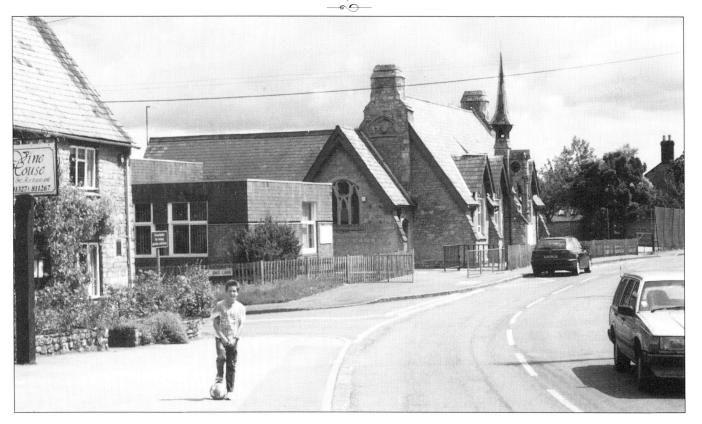

The primary school itself has changed little in the intervening years, but it has expanded considerably. The cottages on the right made way for a larger playground, and the headmaster's house disappeared in the 1960s so that an extension could be built. A few villagers are still employed in agriculture but many now travel daily further afield, returning late in the evening.
(Mollie Dunkley – Paulerspury WI)

Mr Hastilow, owner of the village shop in 1910, pauses before setting out on his rounds, delivering groceries in his pony and trap. On the right a delivery boy sets off on his bicycle. Next door is the Dower House and beyond, two thatched cottages. On the right behind the wall was an orchard – a great scrumping ground for the village lads.

66 *(Margaret Brown – Pitsford WI)*

The last remaining shop in the village became a private house in 1997. Although the shop door has changed, the old bootscraper and slab on the pavement are still there. The thatch roofs are gone, and the orchard was sold in the 1950s. Eight cottages were built, but parts of the old wall can still be seen. Today cars have replaced carts and bicycles – and wheelie-bins have appeared on the pavements at certain times!
(Celia Dobrowolska – Pitsford WI)

In the early 1900s many of the roofs in Ravensthorpe were thatched, soon to be replaced with corrugated iron, earning the village its nickname of 'Tin City'. The cart has been left outside the yard of the old Woolpack public house. The children have to pass the time outside, minding the horse while Father is inside the pub!

(John Patrick – Ravensthorpe WI)

Today's photograph shows that the houses on the left are gone. The pub has closed. Yet on the right there are surprisingly few changes. The small round thatched mud building is gone – the outhouse for a poor old lady whose 'one up one down' was the smallest in the village! The thatched cottage houses the post office. Despite the rough road in the old photograph, essentially the street scene looks reassuringly familiar today.

(Margaret Lewis – Ravensthorpe WI)

69

Rushton High Street

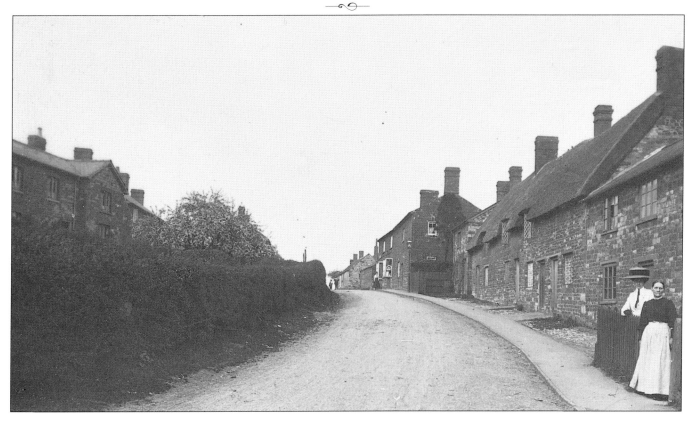

This is Rushton's Tub Row in the early 1900s, now known as the High Street. At the far end were the premises of builders, carpenters and a blacksmith. The bay-windowed house was a bakery. Of the two ladies, the first lost two of her four sons in the First World War. The second, in the hat, was called in by villagers at both ends of life – birth and death.

(Phyllis Turner – Pipewell & Rushton WI)

All the tradesmen's premises are now private houses, the bakery having been also the post office and general stores over the years. The thatched cottages were renovated in 1917 by the then owner of the village, Mr Clarke-Thornhill. The one solitary oil lamp is still to be seen today. It was one of eight. The village now has at least 18 electric street lights. The high hedges have given way to open lawns, driveways and telephone wires.
(Maud Butler – Pipewell & Rushton WI)

71

Staverton, at 500 feet above sea level, is the highest, most westerly village in Northamptonshire. At the turn of the 20th century it was a farming community, the main transport being horse and cart or bicycle. The narrow main road coped with such traffic as there was, which could easily skirt the occasional obstacles.

72 *(Vivien Nunn – Staverton WI)*

DAVENTRY ROAD, STAVERTON

Those thatched cottages were demolished in 1930 to make way for a group of council houses. As motorised traffic increased through the century, many accidents occurred on the road through Staverton, and listed barns suffered damage from the continuous vibration. Much to the relief of villagers, a bypass was built in the 1980s which has made a tremendous improvement to life in this thriving village.
(Vivien Nunn – Staverton WI)

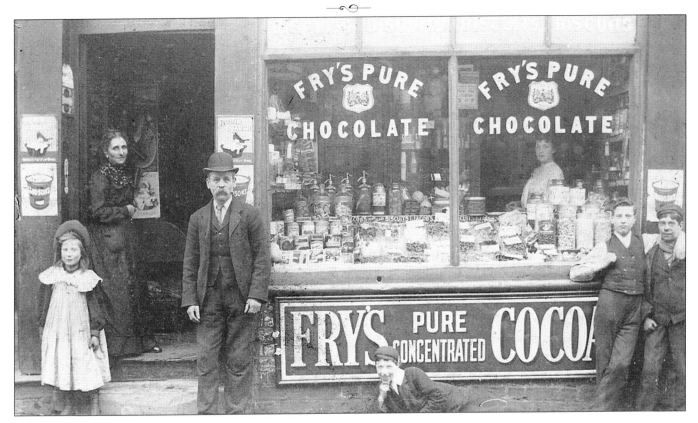

In the early 1900s the proprietor of Sulgrave Stores was Jonas Cleaver, and a descendant of his still lives in the village. In those days there were in addition three pubs, two bakehouses, a wheelwright, a smithy, and various small traders.
(Julie Metcalfe – Sulgrave WI)

The population of Sulgrave, about 370, has stayed almost constant throughout the century but today's photograph shows the one remaining shop and post office combined. It is still a meeting place for all ages. Bottles of sweets are still displayed in the window, but scratch cards are advertised instead of Fry's Cocoa!

(Julie Metcalfe – Sulgrave WI)

THE PLOUGH INN, UPPER BODDINGTON

The licensee of the Plough Inn in 1912 was Herbert Holmes. Later that year Sidney Budd became the landlord, and also provided the local 'taxi' service. He would drive his pony and trap to Fenny Compton station and return with fishermen from Coventry, who then spent the day at Boddington Reservoir. The road surface through the village was local crushed stone.

(Joan Cullen, Mary Clugston – Upper Boddington WI)

THE PLOUGH INN, UPPER BODDINGTON

Sidney Budd was succeeded in 1949 by his daughter Doll, who retired in 1983. The present owners are Mr and Mrs Pears. The thatched building at the side that was the stable and later a milking shed is today the restaurant. The phone box was installed in the late 1940s. The mother of the Nineties pushes the convenient collapsible buggy which can be easily carried in cars. *(Joan Worsley, Mary Clugston – Upper Boddington WI)*

The village derived its name from its three wells, and was known as Well Town. There have been many changes since that time, and since this photograph was taken in about 1910. At the turn of the century Welton had three public houses, two shops, a church and two chapels.

78 *(Val Hamblin – Welton WI)*

Although the number of houses in the village has increased, the population has changed little with approximately 550 inhabitants. Trades have changed considerably however, and the White Horse is the only pub remaining; the two chapels have also gone. Welton still has many beautiful trees thanks to a member of the Clarke family, a renowned horticulturist who developed the clarkia flower and lived in Welton Place, next to the High Street.
(Val Hamblin – Welton WI)

79

Aug. 6th 1917

August 6th 1917 was the date of the August Bank Holiday chapel tea party in Weston, a popular event though on this occasion with a dearth of young men as the war dragged on in France. Tea was laid on in the orchard with access through the barn on the left, from the village street. The chapel is just beyond. The group on the right is standing in front of the village smithy.

80   *(Sheila French – Lois Weedon & Weston WI)*

The barn has been converted to a house and the cottages on the left, which included a laundry and a shop, have gone, replaced by the first new houses to be built in the village for 100 years. The smithy is also a house. Yet three generations of a family which has lived in Weston for nine generations stand where their ancestresses Mrs Mawle and Mrs Middleton stood in 1917 – there is continuity amidst the change.
(Sheila French – Lois Weedon & Weston WI)

Weston by Welland school, seen here in 1910, was built in 1873 and opened with 59 children on the register. The school log records that many of the children were very dull, especially in arithmetic. The school closed in 1960 and today *(inset)* it has been converted into two dwellings, with the next door teacher's house also now a private house. Local children now go to Wilbarston school. The bell tower is to be restored to the roof.

(Sarah Wright – Ashley with Weston by Welland WI)

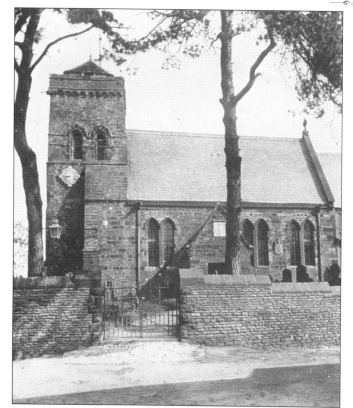

Weston Favell remained a village until the 1920s when new houses began to be built. Until that time fields, allotments and small lakes surrounded the village. Yet St Peter's church remains virtually the same today (*right*), apart from the clock – now round rather than diamond shaped. There was a well to the left of the church gate, now just a gap in the wall.
(*Weston Favell Afternoon WI*)

Taken in about 1900 this photograph shows the centre of Whilton village. To the left the gabled house was an off licence and next door was the bakery, with an entrance for horse and cart between. Across the road is a farmhouse and behind the tree can just be glimpsed another farmhouse and the perimeter of the churchyard wall.

(Janet Bowers – Whilton WI)

Today's Whilton has a population of about 200 and some 80 houses, just slightly less than at the turn of the 20th century. The off licence, the bakery and the farmhouses are all now private houses. The main change over the last 100 years has been the loss of amenities – nowadays the villagers have no pub, shops, post office or transport service.

(Janet Bowers – Whilton WI)

This photograph was taken from Main Street, Wilbarston in about 1918. The Fox public house was then a free house. The chimneyed house belonged to Mrs Patrick, who used one front room as a shop. She also owned a bakehouse behind the house. *(Mrs Joyce Wing – Stoke Albany & Wilbarston WI)*

Today the Fox is still thriving. The old buildings along the road have been demolished to make way for new housing. The shop on the right continues as a post office and general store, but Mrs Patrick's house, and the adjoining tin-roofed barn, were demolished for road widening and the new village green.
(Mr J. Morgan, via Stoke Albany & Wilbarston WI)

Woodford stands on the River Nene, not far from Kettering. At the turn of the 20th century it had a large village green, with the village clearly laid out around it. The village school can be seen to the right. At this time one of the major industries was mining, with ironstone mining, limestone pits and furnaces, and the village was self-sufficient in trades and services.

(Doreen Allen – Woodford Kettering WI)

WOODFORD VILLAGE GREEN

The green is smaller today, cut through by roads, and the war memorial is a reminder of the losses suffered during the 20th century. The old school building is unchanged but it is now used as a closing room for a shoe manufacturer – one of the industries that still supports this busy village. Sadly, only one shop-cum-post office and a fish and chip shop remain from yesterday's traders, though the new school, clubs and pubs, the Baptist chapel and the church are still going strong, the latter with its first female rector.

(Doreen Allen – Woodford Kettering WI)

The Green is the centre of the old village, at the junction of Church Hill, Sunnyside and Green Lane, seen here in 1906. A village pump is to the left, from a time when there was no piped water in the home and water had to be fetched by the bucket. No doubt the local residents were enjoying the unaccustomed novelty of having their photograph taken.

(Janet Montgomery – Wootton WI)

Wootton is now within the Northampton Borough boundary and almost surrounded by housing, with further development in progress. In 1946 the first houses were connected to mains water supplies and soon after the old pump was removed. Yet amidst all this growth, the Wootton Town and Poor Houses Charity, formed in the 19th century, still provides cheap rented accommodation for the needy of the parish – not all things change.
(Janet Montgomery – Wootton WI)

91

THE ELMS, YARDLEY GOBION

It is often the people as well as the buildings who provide continuity over the century. The Elms has been the home of a prominent local farming family at Yardley Gobion for several generations. This picture was taken in about 1905, before the gabled front extension was added. The photographer was standing in the roadway before the house, with the barn close by on the right.

(Betty Wallace – Yardley Gobion WI)

The Elms, Yardley Gobion

Today's photograph clearly shows the busy road that now runs in front of The Elms. It is in the older part of the village, facing Elm Green. The A508 ran through the village until 1989 when its diversion brought welcome relief from the rapidly increasing traffic. The old barn, originally thatched but now tiled, was converted recently to residential accommodation.
(Betty Wallace – Yardley Gobion WI)

BROOKSIDE COTTAGE, YELVERTOFT

Brookside Cottage is probably one of the oldest houses in Yelvertoft, thought to be about 200 years old, and this photograph shows what Brookside Lane looked like early in the century. It was thought to be the original drovers' road to Elkington, reached by crossing the stream via a ford just below the cottage.

(Sheila Smith – Yelvertoft WI)

Brookside Cottage, Yelvertoft

The modern development of Brookside Lane began in 1962, when its name was changed to Ashwells Lane. The cottage has a small amount of cob walling remaining. For many years it was roofed with tin over the thatch, but it has been rethatched in recent years. Despite development, Yelvertoft still retains its rural air.
(Sheila Smith – Yelvertoft WI)

ACKNOWLEDGEMENTS

Contributions for this collection were received from the following WIs, and although not every photograph could be included, without them all this book could not have been produced:

Ashley with Weston by Welland • Barby • Barton Seagrave • Boddington • Boughton • The Bramptons • Braunston • Braybrooke • Brigstock • Bugbrooke • Chacombe • Chelveston cum Caldecott • Clipston • Cold Ashby • Cosgrove• Cranford • Crick • Deanshanger • Earls Barton• Great Doddington • Great Houghton • Greatworth • Greens Norton • Grendon • Gretton • Hargrave • Harlestone • Harpole Evening • The Harrowdens • Hartwell • Holcot • Irchester • Kilsby • King's Sutton • Kislingbury • Lois Weedon and Weston • Long Buckby • Moulton • Nether Heyford • Paulerspury and Alderton • Pipewell and Rushton• Pitsford • Preston Capes • Quinton • Ravensthorpe • Staverton • Stoke Albany and Wilbarston • Sulgrave • Welton • Weston Favell • Whilton • Woodford • Wootton • Yardley Gobion • Yelvertoft.

Cover Photos: The photograph taken in Brigstock in 1905 shows a group of children collecting at the bottom of Grafton Road to go on their annual Sunday school picnic. The track to the left is now a much used road to Kettering. The gas lamp has disappeared, to be replaced by telegraph posts and electricity cables. The cart on the left probably belonged to one of the many carriers who lived in Brigstock at that time. The centre of Brigstock has changed very little structurally and retains much that would be recognised by the children of 1905, as demonstrated by the picture on the back cover. *(Heather Bailey - Brigstock WI)*